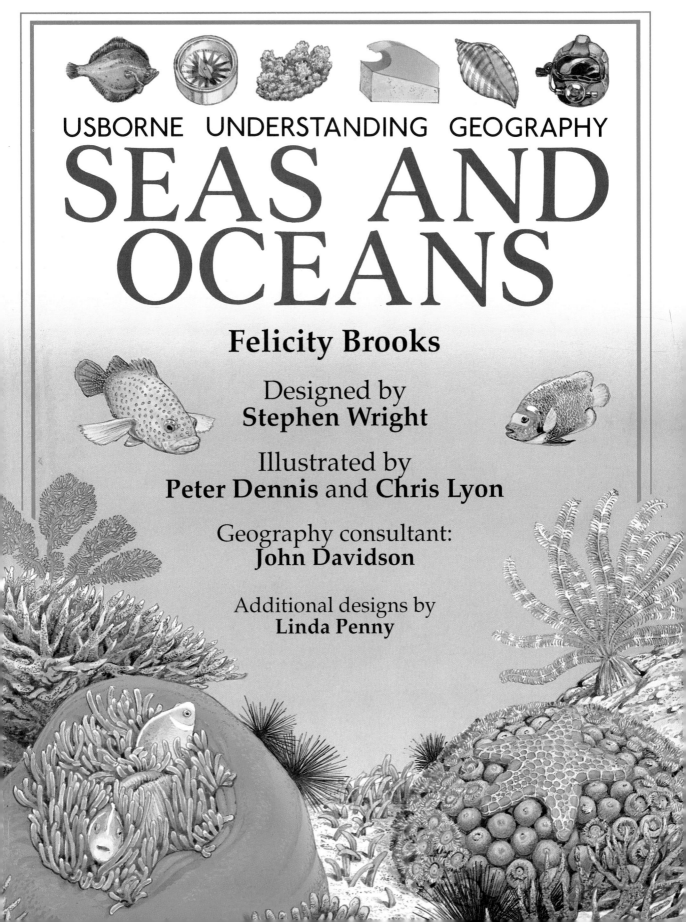

USBORNE UNDERSTANDING GEOGRAPHY
SEAS AND OCEANS

Felicity Brooks

Designed by
Stephen Wright

Illustrated by
Peter Dennis and **Chris Lyon**

Geography consultant:
John Davidson

Additional designs by
Linda Penny

Contents

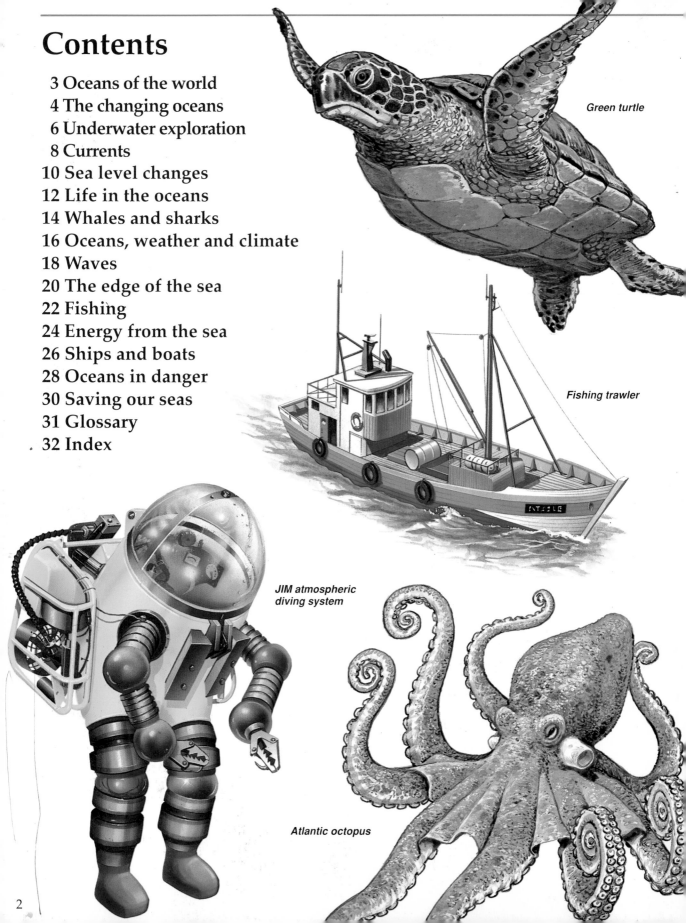

Green turtle

Fishing trawler

JIM atmospheric diving system

Atlantic octopus

Oceans of the world

Seas and oceans cover 71%, or over two-thirds, of the Earth's surface. Most scientists believe that the first living creatures developed in the oceans over 500 million years ago and salt water continues to be a vital habitat for millions of different animals and plants. Oceans help control the Earth's daily weather systems and long-term climate, providing the rain that we need to survive. We also depend on them as a source of food and energy and make use of them in a number of other ways, such as for transport, leisure and for disposal of our waste.

This shows the continent of Antarctica from above the South Pole. Antarctica is surrounded by the Southern Ocean.

This shows the Arctic Ocean from above the North Pole. Over two-thirds of the Arctic Ocean is always covered in ice.

This map shows the world's five oceans and its main seas, bays and gulfs.

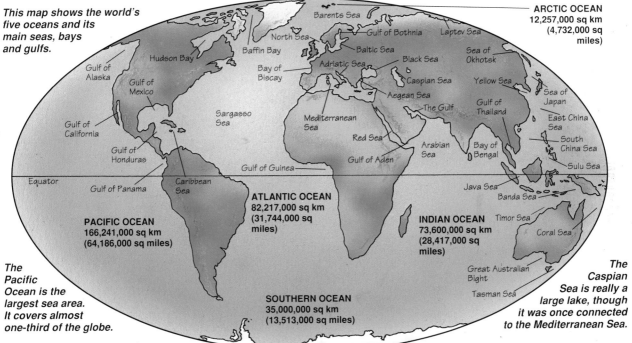

ARCTIC OCEAN
12,257,000 sq km
(4,732,000 sq miles)

ATLANTIC OCEAN
82,217,000 sq km
(31,744,000 sq miles)

PACIFIC OCEAN
166,241,000 sq km
(64,186,000 sq miles)

INDIAN OCEAN
73,600,000 sq km
(28,417,000 sq miles)

SOUTHERN OCEAN
35,000,000 sq km
(13,513,000 sq miles)

The Pacific Ocean is the largest sea area. It covers almost one-third of the globe.

The Caspian Sea is really a large lake, though it was once connected to the Mediterranean Sea.

There are five main oceans - the Pacific, Atlantic, Indian, Arctic and Southern (or Antarctic) Oceans. Each ocean contains smaller areas of water, called seas, bays or gulfs. Many of these are partly surrounded by land. Together, seas and oceans cover an area of over 369 million square kilometres (142 million square miles). All the world's oceans are connected, so sea water flows freely between them.

ATLANTIC OCEAN 22%

PACIFIC OCEAN 45%

INDIAN OCEAN 20%

SOUTHERN OCEAN 9.5%

ARCTIC OCEAN 3.5%

This chart shows how much of the total area of sea water each ocean covers.

The scientific study of seas and oceans is called oceanography. In the past 40 years it has progressed enormously as technology has been developed to allow thorough research and exploration. Oceanographers have now mapped most of the ocean floor and have made many exciting discoveries. Despite these advances, there is still plenty to learn about what has been called "inner space".

The changing oceans

The seas and oceans were not always the shape and size they are today. It is thought that the continents were once joined in one landmass, which scientists call Pangaea, surrounded by one ocean, which they call Panthalassa. The continents then gradually moved apart and new oceans formed.

It is thought that about 200 million years ago there was only one landmass. It probably began to break up about 180 million years ago.

By about 45 million years ago, the outlines of today's continents had begun to take shape. The continents are still on the move today.

If this movement continues at the same rate for another 100 million years, the Atlantic will be the largest ocean and the Mediterranean will disappear.

This movement happens because the Earth is not solid all the way through, as you might imagine, but consists of three main layers - the crust, the mantle and the core. The crust and the upper part of the mantle together are known as the lithosphere. The lithosphere is on average about 100km (62 miles) thick, and solid all the way through. Immediately beneath the lithosphere is the asthenosphere - a layer of hot rock that over long periods can flow slowly.

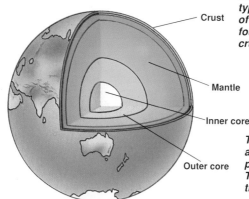

Crust

Mantle

Inner core

Outer core

The crust is solid. There are two types. Oceanic crust is made largely of the rock basalt and is mainly found under oceans. Continental crust forms most of the land.

The mantle is made of dense rock. Its temperature ranges from about 1,000 °C (1,800 °F) to 4,000 °C (7,200 °F).

The core consists mainly of iron and nickel. The outer core is probably melted (molten) metal. The inner core is solid and hotter than 6,000 °C (10,800 °F).

Plates

The lithosphere is broken up into rigid plates which fit together like huge jigsaw pieces. It is thought that the plates move on top of the asthenosphere at a speed of about 5cm (2in) a year. Some plates move apart, some move together and some scrape sideways past each other. As the plates move, the land moves too and the seas and oceans change in size and shape.

This shows the edges, or boundaries, of some of the Earth's plates .

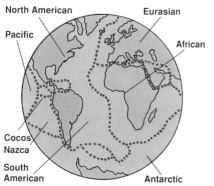

North American

Eurasian

Pacific

African

Cocos

Nazca

South American

Antarctic

How oceans widen

Scientists think that when a plate splits apart, two "new" plates are formed. If the split occurs across land, eventually a new ocean is created. It is thought that the Atlantic Ocean, for example, was formed when North and South America split off from Europe and Africa about 180 million years ago. It is still widening by about 3cm (1.25in) a year along the ridge which runs down the middle. This is how it is thought this may happen.

When a plate starts to split, magma (molten rock) wells up from the mantle. The crust is weakened by the heat, the "new" plates move apart, and a rift valley starts to form.

Magma cools and hardens to form new oceanic crust on the edges of the plates. Eventually, water may flow into the valley and the new crust becomes new ocean floor.

New crust pushes the plates farther apart, so the ocean widens. Older crust on each side of the valley cracks and is lifted up into mountain ranges which form an ocean ridge.

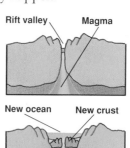

Rift valley   Magma

New ocean   New crust

Ocean ridge

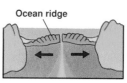

Under the sea

Under the sea, there are vast, flat plains, deep valleys, gently sloping hills, large volcanoes and very deep trenches, as well as ocean ridges. The shallowest parts of the oceans are the continental shelves, where the land slopes gradually down into the water. The deep ocean floor that lies beyond the continental shelves is called the abyssal plain. Here the average depth of the sea is 4km (2.5 miles).

This picture is not to scale.

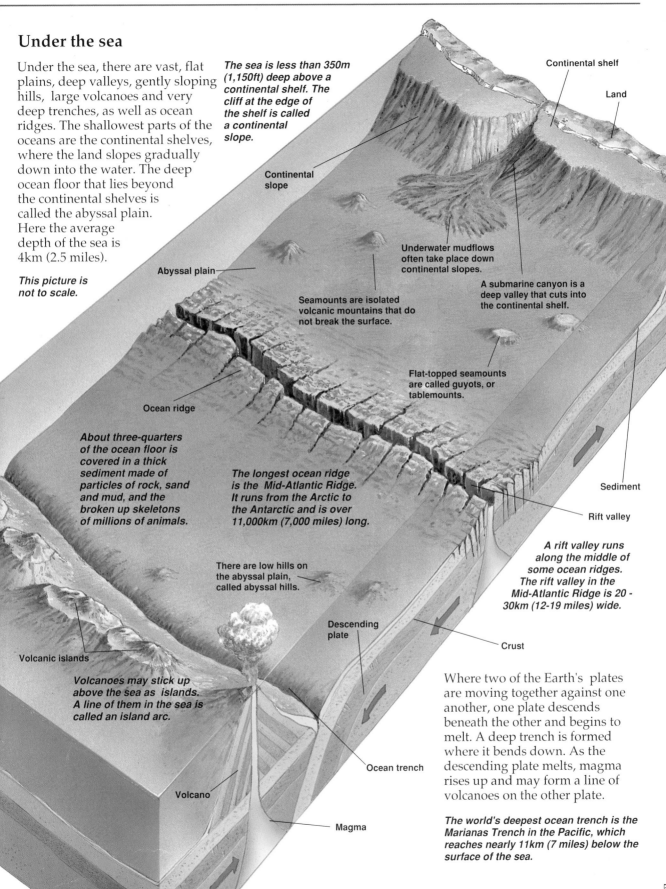

The sea is less than 350m (1,150ft) deep above a continental shelf. The cliff at the edge of the shelf is called a continental slope.

Continental shelf

Land

Continental slope

Underwater mudflows often take place down continental slopes.

A submarine canyon is a deep valley that cuts into the continental shelf.

Abyssal plain

Seamounts are isolated volcanic mountains that do not break the surface.

Flat-topped seamounts are called guyots, or tablemounts.

Ocean ridge

About three-quarters of the ocean floor is covered in a thick sediment made of particles of rock, sand and mud, and the broken up skeletons of millions of animals.

The longest ocean ridge is the Mid-Atlantic Ridge. It runs from the Arctic to the Antarctic and is over 11,000km (7,000 miles) long.

Sediment

Rift valley

A rift valley runs along the middle of some ocean ridges. The rift valley in the Mid-Atlantic Ridge is 20 - 30km (12-19 miles) wide.

There are low hills on the abyssal plain, called abyssal hills.

Descending plate

Crust

Volcanic islands

Volcanoes may stick up above the sea as islands. A line of them in the sea is called an island arc.

Volcano

Ocean trench

Magma

Where two of the Earth's plates are moving together against one another, one plate descends beneath the other and begins to melt. A deep trench is formed where it bends down. As the descending plate melts, magma rises up and may form a line of volcanoes on the other plate.

The world's deepest ocean trench is the Marianas Trench in the Pacific, which reaches nearly 11km (7 miles) below the surface of the sea.

Underwater exploration

People who work under the sea face many problems and dangers. It is dark and cold in the deep ocean, so they must provide their own light and heat as well as equipment for breathing. The deeper you go, the greater the pressure (the weight of water pressing from above) and this causes extra problems.

Diving equipment

In shallow water, divers use SCUBA gear (Self-Contained Underwater Breathing Apparatus), which includes compressed air in cylinders. SCUBA enables divers to go down to 70m (230ft). In deeper water, cylinders are only carried for emergencies. Instead, a diver's breathing gas comes down from the surface, through a tube.

Diver in SCUBA gear

Pressure problems

Down to 50m (165ft), divers can breathe air (21% oxygen, 78% nitrogen). Deeper than this, the pressure makes the nitrogen that dissolves in the blood cause sleepiness and increasing loss of control. Nitrogen can be replaced by helium. Below 90m (295ft), the normal proportion of oxygen can become poisonous, so at these depths, safer, weaker mixtures of oxygen and helium are used.

Even with these safer mixtures, the pressure causes more gas than usual to dissolve in the blood and body tissues. If a diver surfaces quickly, the pressure is reduced too rapidly and the gas may form bubbles in the blood and body tissues, causing a very painful condition called "the bends", which can be fatal. Shallow-water divers avoid the bends by making a slow, controlled return to the surface.

Deep-sea divers have to spend many days inside a decompression chamber where the pressure is reduced very gradually.

Submarines

Inside a submarine, air can be breathed at normal pressure, because a submarine's thick metal walls can withstand the outside water pressure. Large submarines that can stay underwater for weeks are mainly used by the military. Smaller vehicles, which are called submersibles, are used for other work. Most submersibles stay underwater for less than a day.

Submersibles are taken to the site of a dive and lowered into the sea by a "mother ship". This shows the submersible "Alvin" being lowered by its mother ship Atlantis II.

Alvin

The submersible Alvin can dive to a depth of 4,000m (13,100ft). In an emergency, the part containing the crew can separate from the rest, for a quick escape to the surface. Alvin has filmed in the deep ocean around hydrothermal vents (see opposite). It also took the first visitors to the wreck of the Titanic, 73 years after this ship had sunk.

In this picture, part of Alvin has been cut away so that you can see inside. Alvin is only 7.6m (25ft) long.

The crew of two scientists and a pilot rides inside a spherical cabin made of the metal titanium. It is 5cm (2in) thick and able to withstand enormous water pressure.

The cabin is only 2m (7ft) wide. During a dive, the temperature inside may drop to 13°C (55°F).

Telephone and radio equipment allow the crew to keep in contact with the mother ship.

Vertical thrusters can propel Alvin up or down.

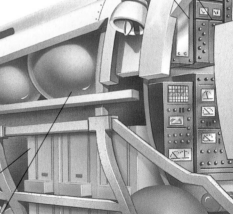

Horizontal thrusters can propel Alvin backward or forward.

Alvin is powered by large, rechargeable batteries.

Pressurized tanks for air. Some contain air for the crew (enough for 3 days). Some are filled with sea water when Alvin needs to sink.

ROVs

Most underwater work is now done by small, unmanned robots called ROVs (Remote Operated Vehicles). They are controlled by a "pilot" on the surface. ROVs can collect samples, take photographs, send back television pictures and perform other fairly complicated tasks.

ROV (Remote Operated Vehicle)

Umbilical carries control signals and power to ROV and TV pictures back to the pilot.

Video camera

Lights

Thrusters for moving around

Arm can hold tools and perform various tasks.

Research ships

Oceanographers often work on ships which are equipped with laboratories, computers and the other equipment that they use for research. RRS Challenger, for example, carries 14 oceanographers who do research in the Atlantic, Mediterranean and Caribbean.

RRS Challenger

Mapping the ocean floor

The seabed can now be mapped by a method called echo-sounding, or sonar. A ship tows a device called a side-scan sonar which sends out pulses of sound over a wide area of the sea floor. The pulses are reflected back as echoes to receivers on the ship, then converted into electrical signals and pictures.

A side-scan sonar sends out sound beams up to 30km (19 miles) on each side of a ship.

Ship

40m (130ft)

Sound scan beam

Side-scan sonar

60km (37 miles)

ALV_N

Sail

The crew enters through a 60cm (2ft) wide hatch.

Camera for taking still photographs

Video camera

Mechanical arms, operated by the crew, collect samples, such as rocks, sediment and sea water.

Lights can illuminate an area up to 12m (40ft) in front.

Acrylic plastic porthole

Basket for samples. Bottles, nets and scoops can be used by the arms.

Hydrothermal vents

A recent underwater discovery has been that of groups of animals, such as giant tube worms, living around hydrothermal vents - hot water springs in the valleys of ocean ridges. They feed on bacteria that live on chemicals which come from the vents.

Giant tube worms grow to 2m (6ft) long.

Vent fish

Currents

The water in the oceans is constantly on the move due to tides, waves and currents. Currents are huge bands of water that flow within the oceans. They may be as warm as 30°C (86°F) or as cold as -2°C (28°F), depending on where they have come from, and over 60km (37 miles) wide. Most move at about 10km (6 miles) per day, though some travel much faster. Currents carry vast amounts of water around the globe, affecting and helping to control the climate (see page 16). There are currents both at the surface and in the deep ocean.

Surface currents

Surface currents affect the top 350m (1,150ft) of the oceans. Scientists still do not fully understand what causes them, or the way in which they affect climate. It is known, however, that the currents are pushed along by the prevailing wind (the most common wind that blows in an area). The rotation of the Earth makes the winds and the ocean surface veer sideways. This is called the Coriolis effect. The direction and strength of currents may also be affected by things such as the shape of landmasses.

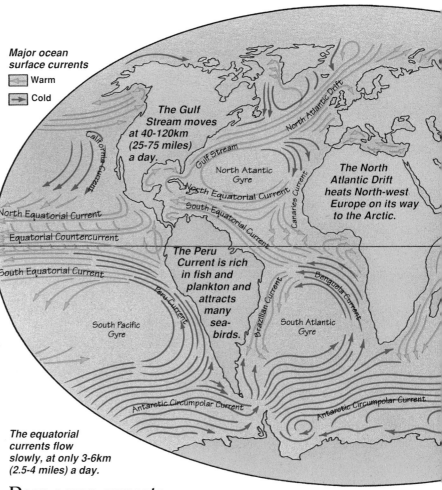

Major ocean surface currents
- Warm
- Cold

The Gulf Stream moves at 40-120km (25-75 miles) a day.

California Current

Gulf Stream

North Atlantic Gyre

North Atlantic Drift

North Equatorial Current

Canaries Current

The North Atlantic Drift heats North-west Europe on its way to the Arctic.

North Equatorial Current

South Equatorial Current

Equatorial Countercurrent

South Equatorial Current

The Peru Current is rich in fish and plankton and attracts many sea-birds.

Peru Current

Brazilian Current

Benguela Current

South Pacific Gyre

South Atlantic Gyre

Antarctic Circumpolar Current

Antarctic Circumpolar Current

The equatorial currents flow slowly, at only 3-6km (2.5-4 miles) a day.

The Coriolis effect - prevailing winds are deflected sideways by the spinning movement of the Earth.

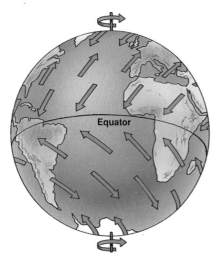

Equator

Deep ocean currents

People have been aware of surface currents for thousands of years, but only recently has the existence of deep, or sub-surface, currents been confirmed. These currents move more slowly and often in the opposite direction to surface currents. They consist of water that is moving away from the poles. When surface currents reach the poles, some of the water freezes, leaving some of its salt in the water that remains. This unfrozen, but very cold water is warmer than the water that is always arriving. It sinks down and creeps along the bottom of the oceans, moving to the equator as a deep current. At the equator, it rises very slowly as it gets warmer, and starts to move back to the poles as a surface current. In this way there is continuous movement between the equator and poles, with deep and surface water moving in opposite directions.

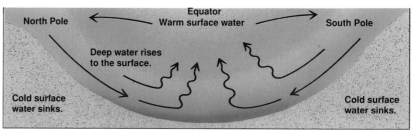

Equator
North Pole ← Warm surface water → South Pole

Deep water rises to the surface.

Cold surface water sinks.

Cold surface water sinks.

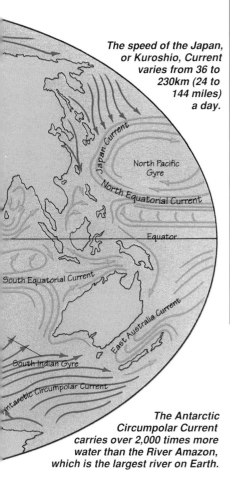

The speed of the Japan, or Kuroshio, Current varies from 36 to 230km (24 to 144 miles) a day.

The Antarctic Circumpolar Current carries over 2,000 times more water than the River Amazon, which is the largest river on Earth.

You can do a simple experiment to show that cold water is heavier than warm water. You will need a clear bowl filled with some warm water and a container of iced water mixed with a little ink.

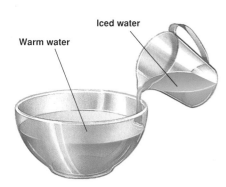

Gently pour the iced water into the bowl. You should notice that it sinks, just as cold water does at the poles.

Gyres

The rotation of the Earth forms the paths of many surface currents into huge loops, called gyres (see map). The North Atlantic Gyre, consists of the Canaries Current, the Gulf Stream and the North Equatorial Current. The strongest currents are on the outside of the gyres.

Gyres spin clockwise in the northern hemisphere and the opposite way in the southern hemisphere.

Carried by currents

If you look at what has been washed up on a beach, you may find things from other countries that have been carried there by currents. Pollution, such as oil, is carried in the same way. Icebergs, sea animals and even land plants may also be carried long distances by currents.

Litter that is washed up on a beach may have been carried long distances by currents.

Seeds may drift a long way with the currents and then take root when they are washed up on the shore.

Eels begin life in the Sargasso Sea and are carried to North America and Europe with the Gulf Stream.

Icebergs drift on polar currents. They may take three years to melt when they reach warmer water.

Measuring currents

Oceanographers use instruments called current meters to measure the temperature, direction and speed of currents. Some types of meters float freely, others are attached to cables. The information is recorded electronically over a period of several months.

A current meter is anchored in the way shown below so that its measurements are not affected by the surface waves.

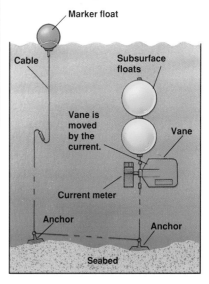

Salt in the sea

Sea water contains about three percent sodium chloride, or common salt, as well as many other chemicals, including traces of gold, silver and even arsenic. Rivers and rain wash salt and other minerals from soil and rocks into the sea. Some minerals also come from underwater volcanoes. When sea water evaporates, its salt is left behind. If you let one litre (1.75 pints) of sea water evaporate, about 35g (1.25oz) of salt is left behind. The salinity of sea water is determined by the amount of salt in it.

Salinity is measured by a salinity meter.

Sea level changes

The level of the sea is always changing. Some changes happen over many years, but some occur daily and are known as tides. The sea rises to its highest level at high tide, then moves back to its lowest level at low tide. Tides are caused mainly by the Moon. As the Moon travels around the Earth, its force of gravity pulls the water nearest to it out in a bulge. The Moon takes 24 hours and 50 minutes to orbit the Earth. During this time there are two high tides and two low tides.

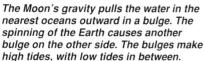

The Moon's gravity pulls the water in the nearest oceans outward in a bulge. The spinning of the Earth causes another bulge on the other side. The bulges make high tides, with low tides in between.

The Sun also exerts a force, but it is weaker than the Moon's because it is farther away. When the Earth, Moon and Sun line up, however, the two forces work together, causing very high tides, known as spring tides. These occur at full moon and new moon.

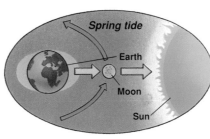

In between spring tides are the very lowest high tides, called neap tides, which occur when the Moon and Sun are at right angles to each other.

The Thames Barrier

When a spring tide occurs at the same time as a storm, a storm surge may occur - water may sweep inland, flooding large areas. This happened in 1953 when waves from the North Sea, pushed by a strong north wind, swept over low-lying areas of the Netherlands, killing over 1,800 people. In Britain, 300 people were killed and parts of East London were flooded as waves surged up the River Thames. Since then, the normal sea level has risen (see page 17), so the Thames Barrier was built to protect London from further floods. It has ten huge gates which are raised when there is a flood threat.

The Thames Barrier spans 520m (one-third of a mile) across the River Thames downstream from central London.

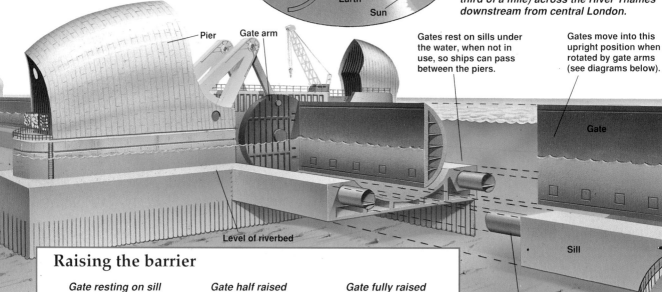

Pier

Gate arm

Gates rest on sills under the water, when not in use, so ships can pass between the piers.

Gates move into this upright position when rotated by gate arms (see diagrams below).

Gate

Level of riverbed

Sill

Raising the barrier

Gate resting on sill

Gate half raised

Gate fully raised

River-bed

Sill

Gate

Tunnels carry drains and control cables between piers and control building on river bank.

Direction of flow of river

Intertidal zones

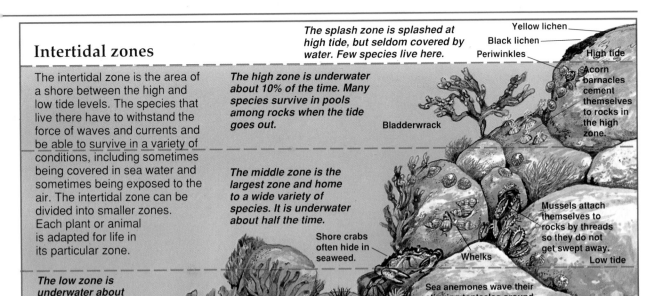

The intertidal zone is the area of a shore between the high and low tide levels. The species that live there have to withstand the force of waves and currents and be able to survive in a variety of conditions, including sometimes being covered in sea water and sometimes being exposed to the air. The intertidal zone can be divided into smaller zones. Each plant or animal is adapted for life in its particular zone.

The splash zone is splashed at high tide, but seldom covered by water. Few species live here.

The high zone is underwater about 10% of the time. Many species survive in pools among rocks when the tide goes out.

The middle zone is the largest zone and home to a wide variety of species. It is underwater about half the time.

The low zone is underwater about 90% of the time and is uncovered only at very low tides.

Yellow lichen
Black lichen
Periwinkles
High tide
Acorn barnacles cement themselves to rocks in the high zone.

Bladderwrack

Mussels attach themselves to rocks by threads so they do not get swept away.
Low tide

Shore crabs often hide in seaweed.

Whelks

Sea anemones wave their stinging tentacles around underwater to catch shrimps and small fish.

Sea urchin

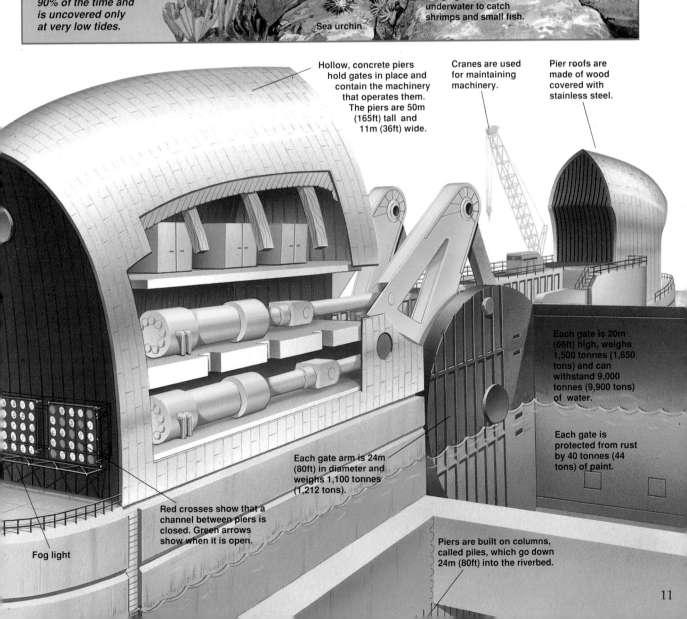

Hollow, concrete piers hold gates in place and contain the machinery that operates them. The piers are 50m (165ft) tall and 11m (36ft) wide.

Cranes are used for maintaining machinery.

Pier roofs are made of wood covered with stainless steel.

Each gate is 20m (66ft) high, weighs 1,500 tonnes (1,650 tons) and can withstand 9,000 tonnes (9,900 tons) of water.

Each gate is protected from rust by 40 tonnes (44 tons) of paint.

Each gate arm is 24m (80ft) in diameter and weighs 1,100 tonnes (1,212 tons).

Red crosses show that a channel between piers is closed. Green arrows show when it is open.

Fog light

Piers are built on columns, called piles, which go down 24m (80ft) into the riverbed.

Life in the oceans

Seas and oceans contain an amazing variety of animals and plants, from the surface all the way down to the trenches. As on land, almost all life depends on plants. The main food supply is billions of microscopic plants, called phytoplankton, which drift with the currents. They use the energy in sunlight to make food for themselves from water, carbon dioxide and minerals. During this process, known as photosynthesis, they produce 70% of the oxygen in the atmosphere.

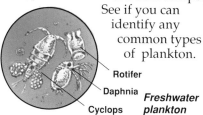

Phytoplankton consist mainly of tiny plants called diatoms. There may be 50,000 of them in a cup of sea water.

Diatoms

Phytoplankton can only live near the surface where there is plenty of sunlight for photosynthesis. Another type of plankton, called zooplankton don't photosynthesize and so can live deeper down. Zooplankton are tiny animals. They feed on phytoplankton or on other zooplankton.

Crab larva
Copepod
Acorn barnacle larva

Zooplankton include the young, or larvae, of crabs, shrimps, jellyfish and fish. Most look nothing like their parents.

Both types of plankton are food for fish and other animals, from small jellyfish to some large species of whales and sharks. Amounts of plankton vary from area to area and season to season. Plankton are found in the greatest numbers above continental shelves and in polar regions.

Krill are a type of zooplankton. The greatest numbers are found in the Southern Ocean.

Plankton live in fresh water too. If you have a chance, study a sample of water from a pond or stream, or some sea water under a microscope. See if you can identify any common types of plankton.

Rotifer
Daphnia
Cyclops
Freshwater plankton

Food webs and pyramids

Animals eat plants or other animals and may themselves be consumed by other species. Over 90 percent of all sea creatures end up being eaten. All life in the oceans is linked in this way in a vast food web, based on phytoplankton. Because so many small plants and animals are needed to feed larger ones, there are always fewer large animals in the sea than small ones. One way of showing this is as a food pyramid.

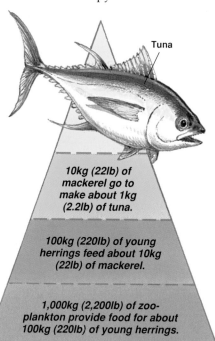

Tuna

10kg (22lb) of mackerel go to make about 1kg (2.2lb) of tuna.

100kg (220lb) of young herrings feed about 10kg (22lb) of mackerel.

1,000kg (2,200lb) of zooplankton provide food for about 100kg (220lb) of young herrings.

10,000kg (22,000lb) of phytoplankton provide food for about 1,000kg (2,200lb) of zooplankton.

Ocean layers

The ocean can be divided into various layers, called zones, according to the amount of light and heat that penetrate from the surface. The temperature and the amount of light decrease with depth. All the plants and most of the animals are found in the top two zones.

This picture is not to scale.

Sea level
Continental shelf

The sunlit, or euphotic, zone is home to all the plants and a wide variety of animals.

Phytoplankton
Zooplankton

Herrings

In the twilight, or mesopelagic, zone only a little light penetrates from above. Its largest inhabitants are fish, squid and octopuses.

Octopus

In the bathypelagic, or sunless, zone the temperature is about 4°C (39°F). Animals mainly feed on a "rain" of dead plankton that sinks down from above.

In the abyssal zone, it is dark and the water is icy cold. The few animals that are found there have to live with constant high pressure.

Animals in ocean trenches may be over 6km (4 miles) from the surface. They rely on food that sinks down from above.

Sponges

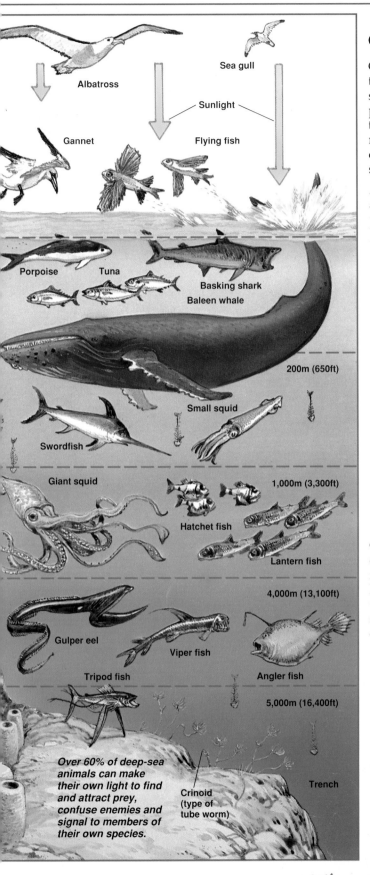

Albatross

Sea gull

Sunlight

Gannet

Flying fish

Porpoise   Tuna

Basking shark

Baleen whale

200m (650ft)

Swordfish

Small squid

Giant squid

1,000m (3,300ft)

Hatchet fish

Lantern fish

4,000m (13,100ft)

Gulper eel

Viper fish

Tripod fish

Angler fish

5,000m (16,400ft)

Over 60% of deep-sea animals can make their own light to find and attract prey, confuse enemies and signal to members of their own species.

Crinoid (type of tube worm)

Trench

Coral reefs

Coral reefs are found in warm, shallow, clear, tropical water. They are made of the skeletons of small animals called coral polyps. When old polyps die, new ones start to grow on top of their skeletons. The oldest reefs started to form many thousands of years ago. One type of reef, called an atoll, is ring-shaped or horseshoe-shaped. This is how it is thought an atoll forms.

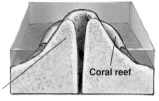

A coral reef starts to grow around a volcanic island. The island then starts to sink into the rocks of the ocean floor when volcanic activity has finished.

Coral reef

Sinking volcanic island

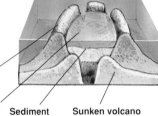

The reef keeps growing upward as the island continues to sink, so that the reef encloses a lagoon (a shallow, saltwater lake).

Coral reef

Island

Lagoon

When the island has sunk completely, the reef that is left is known as an atoll - a circular reef with a lagoon inside.

Atoll

Lagoon

Sediment   Sunken volcano

Coral reefs hold a greater variety of life than other parts of the ocean, including a third of all fish species. The largest reef is the Great Barrier Reef off the east coast of Australia. It is 2,027km (1,260 miles) long and home to 3,000 species of animals, including 350 corals and 2,000 species of fish.

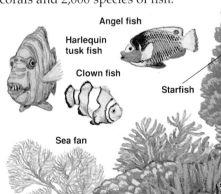

Angel fish

Harlequin tusk fish

Clown fish

Starfish

Sea fan

Giant clam

Whales and sharks

Whales are sea mammals that give birth to live young. They can dive deep down into the ocean, but must return to the surface frequently because they need to breathe air. They have large, complex brains and a thick layer of fat, called blubber, under their skin which stores energy and helps stop their body heat from escaping. They swim by moving their tails up and down. There are at least 80 known species of whales in two main groups: toothed whales and baleen whales.

Baleen whales

Baleen whales include blue whales, fin whales, humpback whales and gray whales. They all eat plankton (especially krill), and some also feed on small fish. They have a fringe of tough bristles, called baleen, which grows down from the gums of their upper jaws. The baleen is used to strain plankton from the water.

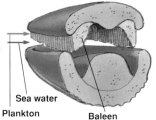

A baleen whale takes an enormous gulp of sea water that contains plankton. It then closes its mouth.

Sea water

Plankton

Baleen

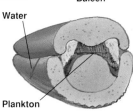

Water

The sea water is then forced out through the baleen, trapping the plankton which the whale swallows.

Plankton

Humpback whales can grow to 16m (53ft) and weigh 46 tonnes (50 tons). They gather in groups for breeding or feeding. The males are famed for their "songs". They dive to a depth of 24m (80ft) and sing loud, slow songs that last 30 minutes or more and may be repeated many times. No one knows exactly why they do this, but it may be to impress females.

Humpback whales sometimes propel themselves out of the sea and fall back with a splash. This is called breaching.

Toothed whales

Toothed whales, such as sperm whales, orcas (killer whales) and the 32 members of the dolphin family are generally smaller than baleen whales. They have sharp, cone-shaped teeth and live mainly on fish, squid and octopuses. They can locate animals and objects by sending out rapid clicks which bounce off the object or animal and back to them.

Sperm whales are the largest toothed whales. They can dive as deep as 3,000m (9,900ft) and stay underwater for over an hour.

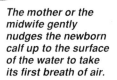

Sperm whales are often covered in scars from fights with giant squid.

Female bottle-nosed dolphins give birth every 2-3 years. A "midwife" often helps the mother. A calf is born tail first.

The calf has its eyes open and can swim perfectly as soon as it is born. The mother or midwife quickly severs the umbilical cord.

The mother or the midwife gently nudges the newborn calf up to the surface of the water to take its first breath of air.

The calf swims next to its mother and feeds from her for about 18 months. Dolphins are very protective of their young.

About every 20 minutes the calf dives down to feed on rich milk from milk ducts near its mother's tail.

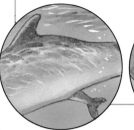
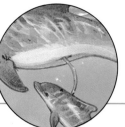

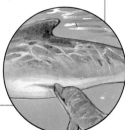

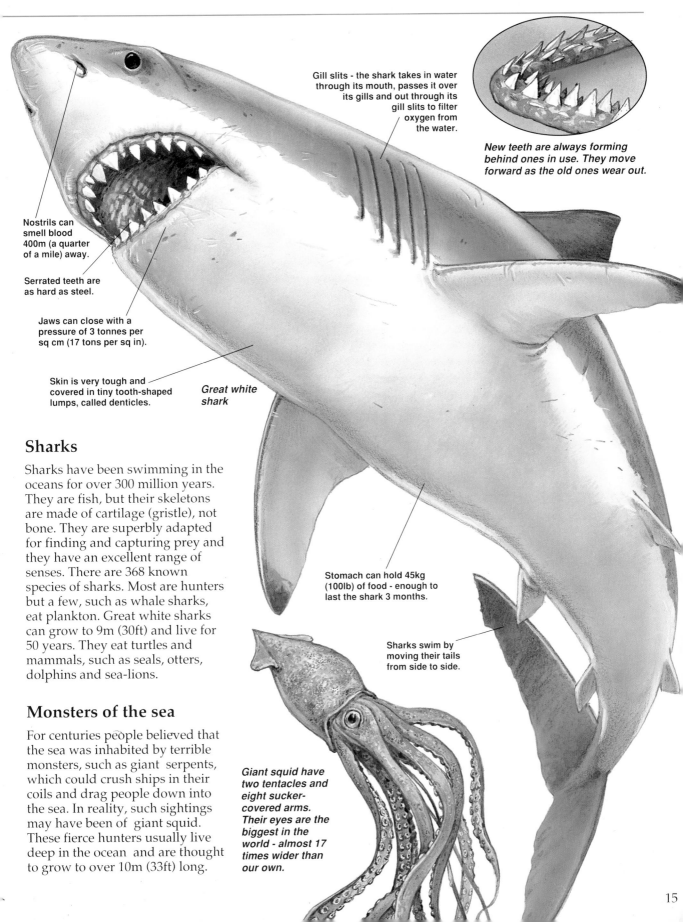

Gill slits - the shark takes in water through its mouth, passes it over its gills and out through its gill slits to filter oxygen from the water.

New teeth are always forming behind ones in use. They move forward as the old ones wear out.

Nostrils can smell blood 400m (a quarter of a mile) away.

Serrated teeth are as hard as steel.

Jaws can close with a pressure of 3 tonnes per sq cm (17 tons per sq in).

Skin is very tough and covered in tiny tooth-shaped lumps, called denticles.

Great white shark

Sharks

Sharks have been swimming in the oceans for over 300 million years. They are fish, but their skeletons are made of cartilage (gristle), not bone. They are superbly adapted for finding and capturing prey and they have an excellent range of senses. There are 368 known species of sharks. Most are hunters but a few, such as whale sharks, eat plankton. Great white sharks can grow to 9m (30ft) and live for 50 years. They eat turtles and mammals, such as seals, otters, dolphins and sea-lions.

Monsters of the sea

For centuries people believed that the sea was inhabited by terrible monsters, such as giant serpents, which could crush ships in their coils and drag people down into the sea. In reality, such sightings may have been of giant squid. These fierce hunters usually live deep in the ocean and are thought to grow to over 10m (33ft) long.

Stomach can hold 45kg (100lb) of food - enough to last the shark 3 months.

Sharks swim by moving their tails from side to side.

Giant squid have two tentacles and eight sucker-covered arms. Their eyes are the biggest in the world - almost 17 times wider than our own.

Oceans, weather and climate

The oceans hold 97 percent of the world's water and have a greater effect on weather and climate than any other feature on Earth. They release vast amounts of moisture into the air, which helps to generate rain, snow and hail. The continual movement of water between sea, air and land is called the hydrologic cycle, or water cycle.

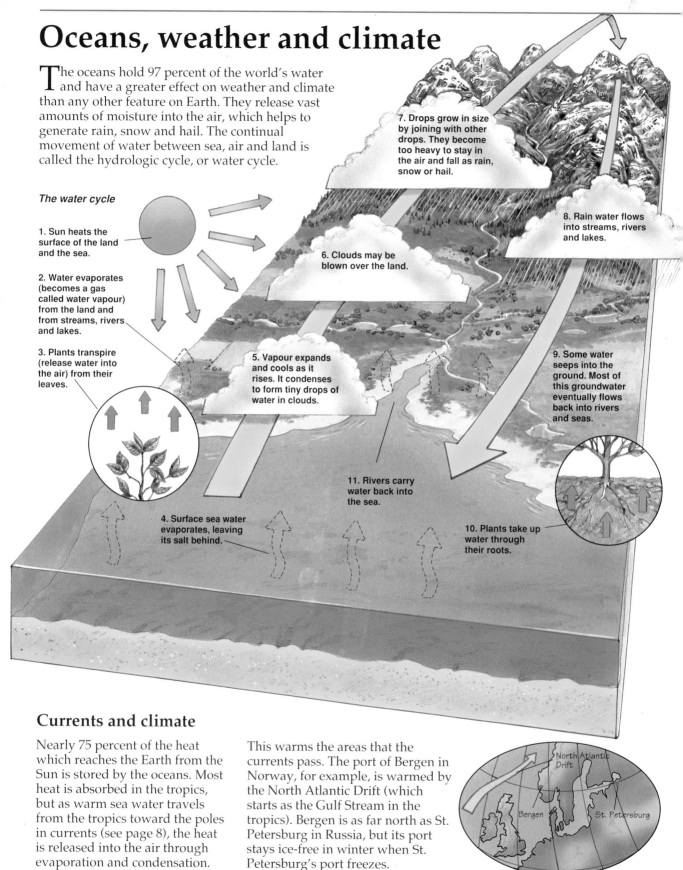

The water cycle

1. Sun heats the surface of the land and the sea.

2. Water evaporates (becomes a gas called water vapour) from the land and from streams, rivers and lakes.

3. Plants transpire (release water into the air) from their leaves.

4. Surface sea water evaporates, leaving its salt behind.

5. Vapour expands and cools as it rises. It condenses to form tiny drops of water in clouds.

6. Clouds may be blown over the land.

7. Drops grow in size by joining with other drops. They become too heavy to stay in the air and fall as rain, snow or hail.

8. Rain water flows into streams, rivers and lakes.

9. Some water seeps into the ground. Most of this groundwater eventually flows back into rivers and seas.

10. Plants take up water through their roots.

11. Rivers carry water back into the sea.

Currents and climate

Nearly 75 percent of the heat which reaches the Earth from the Sun is stored by the oceans. Most heat is absorbed in the tropics, but as warm sea water travels from the tropics toward the poles in currents (see page 8), the heat is released into the air through evaporation and condensation.

This warms the areas that the currents pass. The port of Bergen in Norway, for example, is warmed by the North Atlantic Drift (which starts as the Gulf Stream in the tropics). Bergen is as far north as St. Petersburg in Russia, but its port stays ice-free in winter when St. Petersburg's port freezes.

Satellites

Satellites in space are used to measure the temperature of the sea. Using instruments which are sensitive to infrared light, they can produce images which show the temperatures of the water surface. Warm and cold currents are clearly visible on these images.

Satellite image from ERS-1 (European Remote Sensing) satellite. The warmest areas are shown in red.

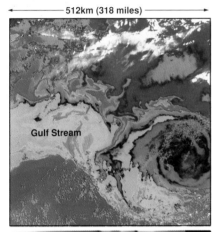

← 512km (318 miles) →

Gulf Stream

6°C (42°F)	10°C (50°F)	14°C (57°F)	19°C (66°F)	23°C (73°F)

El Niño

Every few years, a warm current, known as El Niño, occurs off the west coast of South America when the prevailing southeasterly wind (which usually causes cold water to well up from the deep ocean) dies down. Nobody knows why this happens, but it has a devastating effect on weather and wildlife. Plankton, fish and the birds that feed on them die or disappear.

El Niño's heat and moisture bring heavy rain and floods to regions which are usually dry and cool.

Storms from the sea

Tropical cyclones (also known as hurricanes, typhoons or willy-willies) are huge, circular storms with winds of over 120km (75 miles) per hour, heavy rain and a ring of clouds that can be over 480km (300 miles) wide. They only develop over open oceans with a surface temperature higher than 27°C (80°F). Tropical cyclones break up quickly if they move over the land, but not usually before causing enormous damage.

Hurricanes can be tracked by satellite, but it is difficult to forecast their exact path. This image shows Hurricane Gilbert over the Gulf of Mexico in 1988.

Rising and falling levels

Throughout history, sea levels have fallen and risen as the climate and the size and shape of the oceans have changed (see page 4). A ruined temple in Italy provides evidence of this. It was built near the shore, over 2,000 years ago. Since then it has been underwater for many years before coming back onto dry land as the sea level fell.

This picture shows the Temple of Jupiter at Pozzuoli in Italy. The marks on the columns were made by sea plants and animals during the years that the temple was underwater.

The average level of all the seas and oceans has risen by 10-20cm (4-8in) since 1900. It is thought this is due to expansion of sea water and glaciers melting as the world has become warmer by about 0.5°C (1°F). This warming (known as global warming) may be part of a natural cycle; the atmosphere has warmed and cooled many times in the past. However, it is also partly due to higher levels of polluting "greenhouse" gases, such as carbon dioxide in the atmosphere, which come from burning fossil fuels such as coal and oil.

Global warming

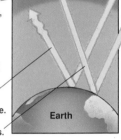

Heat from the Sun enters atmosphere, passing through "greenhouse" gases.

Some radiated and reflected heat is absorbed by these gases, raising the Earth's temperature.

Earth

Some heat escapes.

Many experts predict a further temperature rise of 2-3°C (4-6°F) by the year 2050 and a sea level rise of 30cm (1ft), although this is by no means certain. Such a rise could cause flooding of large areas of low-lying land and this would have a serious impact on people and wildlife. Another result of global warming might be an increased number of storms such as tropical cyclones.

Waves

Most waves are formed by wind blowing across the surface of the sea. Their size and power depends on the wind's speed and the length of time and distance that it has blown over the sea. The distance over which a wind blows is called the fetch. The Pacific has the greatest fetch and so produces the biggest waves. Waves that break on the Pacific coast of the US may have begun 10,000km (6,200 miles) away.

Wave shapes

Unlike currents and tides, waves in the open ocean do not move the water forward at all. The waves travel, but the water doesn't. You can see this if you watch something such as a bird, bobbing up and down on the sea.

A bird is not moved forward by a passing wave .

A wave makes particles of water move around and around in circles. The circles are smaller and smaller the farther down they are from the surface, until a wave has no effect on the water at all. If you were in a submarine more than 100m (330ft) down, you would not notice the effect of waves, even with a fierce storm above.

Breaking waves

When a wave approaches a sloping beach, the water starts to drag on the seabed. The water particles move in flatter and flatter ovals and this slows the wave down. When the wave reaches very shallow water, the particles can no longer complete their ovals and the wave's crest (top)

topples over and breaks on the shore. A breaking wave may spill, plunge or surge onto the shore, depending on the steepness of the underwater slope.

With a gentle slope, waves break before reaching the shore and spill water onto it.

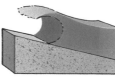

If there is a steep slope, waves plunge onto the shore.

On a very steep beach, waves surge onto the shore.

The work of waves

Waves can travel long distances without changing shape or losing energy, long after the wind that originally created them has died away. When they do finally break on the shore, waves release energy that has been stored up during their journey. The force of waves continuously breaking is constantly reshaping the land

around the coasts in various ways.

Waves which surge or spill onto the beach gradually build it up and so are called constructive waves (see pages 20-21). Waves which plunge onto the shore are called destructive waves because they slowly erode, or wear away, the land at the coasts and remove beaches that protect the land.

(see pages 20-21)

Wave words

The foaming water which runs up a beach is called **swash**.

Water returning down a beach is called **backwash**.

The highest point of a wave is called its **crest**.

The lowest point between two waves is called a **trough**.

Wave period is the time between one wave and the next.

Wave height is the vertical distance between a crest and trough.

Wavelength is the distance between the crest of one wave and the next.

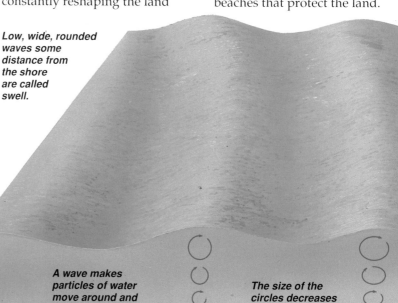

Low, wide, rounded waves some distance from the shore are called swell.

A wave makes particles of water move around and around in circles.

The size of the circles decreases with depth.

Destructive waves

Destructive waves slowly drag away the sand and shingle (small pebbles) that form beaches. They hurl the weight of their water and this beach material onto rocks and cliffs, eroding their surfaces. They force water and air into every crack and crevice, often with explosive power, gradually widening and weakening the rocks. Pieces of rock that break off are used for further erosion. In this way even very hard rock is slowly worn away and the land at the edge of the sea is shaped by the waves.

Disappearing villages

Waves can erode land surprisingly fast. For example, the coast of Holderness in Lincolnshire, England is being eroded at an average rate of about 2m (6ft) a year. 50 villages that were mentioned in the Domesday Book of 1086 have since disappeared.

Since North America's tallest lighthouse was built at Cape Hatteras in 1870, more than 426m (1,400ft) of the beach has been worn away.

Tsunami

Tsunami (sometimes wrongly called tidal waves) are waves that can do terrible damage. They are caused by underwater earthquakes or volcanic eruptions and can cross oceans faster than a jet plane at 1,000km (620 miles) per hour. In deep water, they may be less than 1m (3ft) tall, but if they approach land, they slow down and their height may increase dramatically to 30-50m (100-165ft), before they crash down, surge inland and destroy everything in their path. Ninety percent of all recorded tsunami have occurred in the Pacific.

Headlands are formed by areas of resistant rock which have been eroded more slowly than the surrounding less resistant rock.

Sometimes waves force open a vertical crack leading up from the top of a cave, which opens up a blowhole on the top a cliff.

The blasting action of waves enlarges cracks in the cliff, eventually forming caves.

An arch is formed when waves erode caves on either side of a headland until they meet.

High, steep waves may erode a cliff at its base, forming a wave-cut notch. The cliff may eventually be weakened so much that it collapses.

A wave-cut platform, or terrace, is all that is left of cliffs that have been eroded by waves.

A stack forms when the top of an arch is weakened so much that it collapses into the sea. A stack may be eroded at its base. Eventually its top falls off, leaving a stump.

Headland
Blowhole
Wave-cut notch
Cave
Wave-cut platform
Headland
Stack
Stump
Arch
Cliff
Beach

Pebbles, shingle or sand on a beach are the result of erosion.

Water particles move in flatter and flatter ovals as a wave approaches a sloping beach.

Waves get steeper and closer together as they near the shore.

In shallow water, the particles can no longer complete their ovals, so a wave breaks.

The edge of the sea

While parts of a coast are being eroded, other parts are being added to, or built up. This process is called deposition. It occurs where constructive waves surge or spill onto a shore (see page 18). The incoming waves carry beach material, such as pebbles, shingle and sand onto the shore and deposit it there. This gradually builds beaches and some other coastal features.

Longshore drift

In places where waves, driven by a prevailing wind, usually meet a beach at an angle, beach material may move steadily along the shore. This happens because the material is carried up and along the beach at an angle by the swash, but is dragged straight down by the backwash. This zig-zagging movement of material along a shore is called longshore drift or longshore flow.

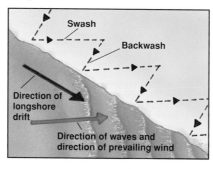

Swash

Backwash

Direction of longshore drift

Direction of waves and direction of prevailing wind

Longshore drift may continue off the end of a beach where the angle of the coast changes, eventually forming a spit (see picture below).

In addition, at a headland, river mouth or bay, waves slow down and cannot carry as much material as when they were moving fast, so some of it is dropped, or deposited. The material gradually builds up on the seabed and may eventually stick up above sea level, to form some of the features which are shown below.

Rivers also help to build new land by carrying mud down to the sea. Where they meet tidal water in an estuary, they deposit this mud to form mud flats.

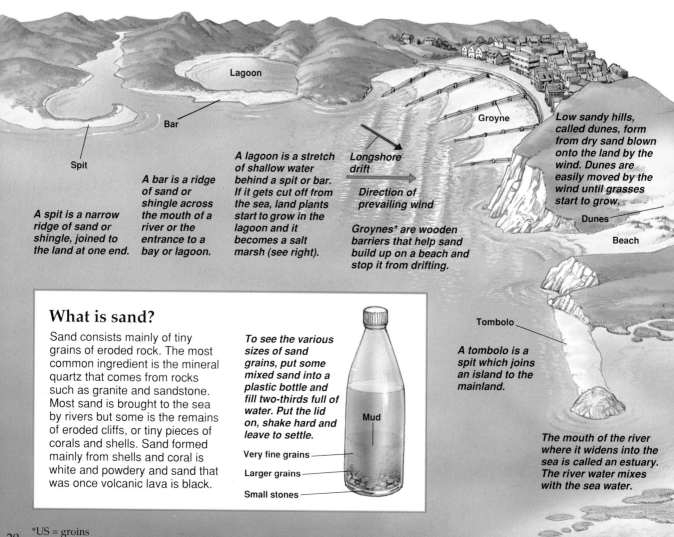

Lagoon

Bar

Groyne

Spit

A spit is a narrow ridge of sand or shingle, joined to the land at one end.

A bar is a ridge of sand or shingle across the mouth of a river or the entrance to a bay or lagoon.

A lagoon is a stretch of shallow water behind a spit or bar. If it gets cut off from the sea, land plants start to grow in the lagoon and it becomes a salt marsh (see right).

Longshore drift

Direction of prevailing wind

Groynes* are wooden barriers that help sand build up on a beach and stop it from drifting.

Low sandy hills, called dunes, form from dry sand blown onto the land by the wind. Dunes are easily moved by the wind until grasses start to grow.

Dunes

Beach

Tombolo

A tombolo is a spit which joins an island to the mainland.

The mouth of the river where it widens into the sea is called an estuary. The river water mixes with the sea water.

What is sand?

Sand consists mainly of tiny grains of eroded rock. The most common ingredient is the mineral quartz that comes from rocks such as granite and sandstone. Most sand is brought to the sea by rivers but some is the remains of eroded cliffs, or tiny pieces of corals and shells. Sand formed mainly from shells and coral is white and powdery and sand that was once volcanic lava is black.

To see the various sizes of sand grains, put some mixed sand into a plastic bottle and fill two-thirds full of water. Put the lid on, shake hard and leave to settle.

Mud

Very fine grains

Larger grains

Small stones

*US = groins

Salt marshes

If plants begin to grow on a mud flat, their roots help hold the mud in place and more mud is trapped. Eventually this forms a marsh, called a salt marsh (because the water is salty). Salt marshes also form behind spits and in lagoons behind bars.

Salt marshes are regularly covered by tides. The plants that grow there can survive with their roots in mud which has a lot of salt and little oxygen in it. Cordgrass, for example, can filter out most of the salt from the water entering its roots. Any salt that does seep through is excreted (passed out) through pores (holes) on its leaves and stems. These pores can also take in oxygen from the air and pass it down to the roots buried in mud.

Salt on cordgrass, excreted by pores

Salt marshes form on mud flats when plants begin to grow.

Salt marshes are broken up by creeks and channels through which tidal waters flow.

Salt marsh plants and zones

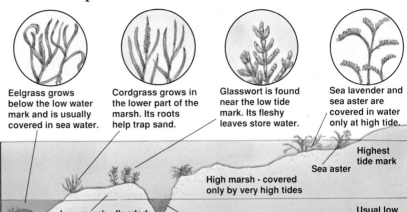

Eelgrass grows below the low water mark and is usually covered in sea water.

Cordgrass grows in the lower part of the marsh. Its roots help trap sand.

Glasswort is found near the low tide mark. Its fleshy leaves store water.

Sea lavender and sea aster are covered in water only at high tide.

Highest tide mark

Sea aster

High marsh - covered only by very high tides

Low marsh - flooded by every high tide

Creek

Usual low tide mark

Mangrove swamps

In the tropics, salt marshes and grasses are replaced by mangrove swamps and mangrove trees. The trees excrete excess salt from glands on the underside of their leaves. They also have roots which stick up above the mud and take in oxygen. Mangrove swamps are important as nurseries for young shellfish and many other animals.

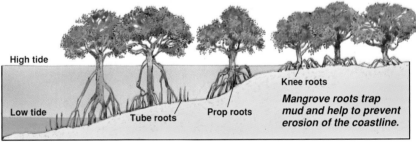

High tide

Low tide

Tube roots

Prop roots

Knee roots

Mangrove roots trap mud and help to prevent erosion of the coastline.

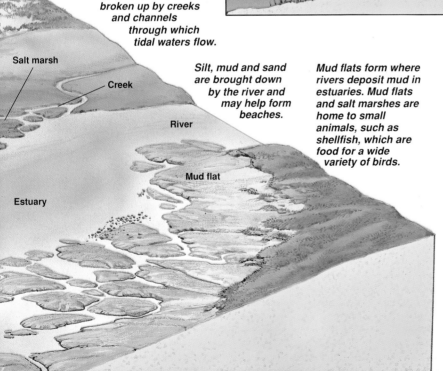

Salt marsh

Creek

River

Mud flat

Estuary

Silt, mud and sand are brought down by the river and may help form beaches.

Mud flats form where rivers deposit mud in estuaries. Mud flats and salt marshes are home to small animals, such as shellfish, which are food for a wide variety of birds.

Mangrove seeds

Seeds of red mangrove trees grow into seedlings while still attached to the parent trees.

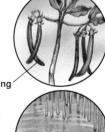

Seedling

When a seedling falls from the tree it can float in the salty water for up to 12 months before it implants in the mud.

A seedling can grow fast when it implants, anchoring itself firmly before the tide can sweep it away.

Fishing

The seas and oceans have been a very important source of food for thousands of years. Today over 75 million tonnes (83 million tons) of fish and shellfish are caught each year around the world. About two-thirds of this catch is for direct human consumption. The rest is made into animal feed, fertilizer, or fish oil which is used in the manufacture of products such as paint, glue and soap.

How the world's fish are used

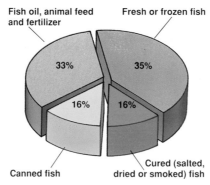

Fish oil, animal feed and fertilizer

Fresh or frozen fish

33%

35%

16%

16%

Canned fish

Cured (salted, dried or smoked) fish

Modern methods

Modern trawlers (fishing boats) use echo-sounders (see page 7) to find fish, so fishermen know exactly where to cast their nets. Huge factory trawlers stay at sea for months at a time and can process vast quantities of fish. The fish are cleaned and filleted on board the trawler and then frozen or canned. Leftover parts are made into fish oil or fish meal for fertilizers or animal feed.

Factory trawler

Groups of fish

Of the 20,000 known species of fish, only about 22 species are fished commercially. Sea fish are divided into three main groups: demersal, pelagic and shellfish.

Demersal fish live near the seabed. Pelagic fish swim in shoals nearer to the surface in the open ocean. Shellfish are found on the seabed or near the shore.

Pelagic fish include tuna, sardines and swordfish as well as the species shown below.

Demersal fish include cod, haddock, whiting, Alaskan pollack, sole and turbot in addition to these species.

Shellfish include crabs, clams, oysters and scallops, as well as lobsters, mussels, shrimps and prawns.

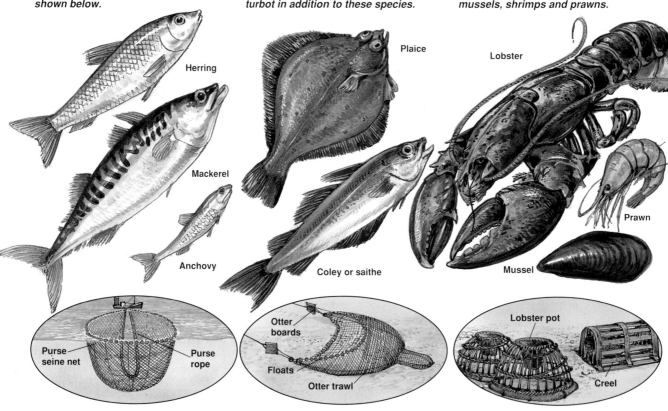

Herring

Mackerel

Anchovy

Plaice

Coley or saithe

Lobster

Prawn

Mussel

Purse seine net

Purse rope

Otter boards

Floats

Otter trawl

Lobster pot

Creel

Purse seine nets, which can encircle a shoal, are used in pelagic fishing. They close up around the fish when the purse rope is pulled from above.

Large nets called otter trawls are mainly used in demersal fishing. They are dragged along the seabed, kept open by pieces of wood called otter boards.

Various different methods are used to catch shellfish. Pots and creels, baited with fish or fish heads, are used to catch crabs and lobsters.

Overfishing

Advances in fishing technology, huge nets and powerful trawlers mean that more than 200 tonnes (220 tons) of fish can now be landed in a single catch. In many areas of the world this has led to overfishing - a serious reduction in the number of fish able to breed left in the sea. This map shows some of the species at risk.

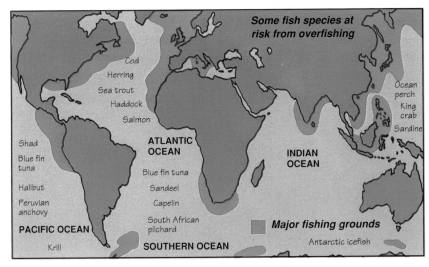

Some fish species at risk from overfishing

Cod
Herring
Sea trout
Haddock
Salmon
Ocean perch
King crab
Sardine

Shad
Blue fin tuna
Halibut
Peruvian anchovy

ATLANTIC OCEAN
Blue fin tuna
Sandeel
Capelin
South African pilchard

PACIFIC OCEAN
Krill

INDIAN OCEAN

Major fishing grounds
Antarctic icefish

SOUTHERN OCEAN

Limits to fishing

These are some ways of tackling the problems of overfishing and the threats to sea animals and birds caused by fishing.

★Quotas - limits on how many fish of each species each country may catch each year. When the total has been reached, any fish that are then caught must be thrown back.

★Limits on how many boats are allowed to fish, where they may fish and how many days of the year they can go out to sea.

★Restrictions on the size of fish that may be caught. (Small, young fish must be thrown back).

★Regulating the type of nets that can be used and the size of the holes in them. Nets with larger holes allow young fish to escape.

Threats to wildlife

Overfishing disrupts the food web (see page 12) and causes problems for fish-eating animals, such as birds, dolphins and seals. When sandeels, for example, were overfished around the Shetland Islands in Scotland in the mid-1980s, puffins were deprived of food for their young and many puffin chicks starved to death as a direct result.

Puffin with sandeels

Another consequence of fishing is the accidental entanglement of sea animals in fishing nets. Seals, dolphins, turtles and seabirds get caught in many types of fishing net and in pieces of damaged nets that fishermen cut out and throw over-board from trawlers when they are making repairs to nets.

A piece of discarded fishing net around the neck of a Cape fur seal pup. Many thousands of animals die every year as a result of accidental entanglement in nets.

Farming fish

Fish such as salmon and tuna can be bred in pens, or cages, moored to the seabed. They are fed high-protein pellets to make them grow fast. Fish farming was seen as a way of relieving pressure on wild fish stocks, but as this industry has grown, it has caused further problems. Chemicals added to the pens to control diseases can wash into the sea and kill wildlife. When fish escape (as happened in 1988 when two million salmon escaped from farms in Norway) they can spread disease to wild fish. Also, a lot of food for farmed fish comes from wild sea species. Over 3 tonnes (3.3 tons) of sandeels need to be made into food pellets for each tonne (1.1 ton) of salmon produced by a farm.

Salmon are bred in pens in fish farms in the sea. Such farms can cause environmental damage.

Energy from the sea

Almost two-thirds of the world's energy comes from oil and natural gas which are extracted from under the seabed or under the ground. Nearly a third of the world's oil and large amounts of gas come from offshore fields. Oil and gas are described as non-renewable energy resources, because they will one day run out. The oceans are also a potential source of renewable energy, if methods can be found to tap it.

The origins of oil

Oil and gas are formed mainly from the remains of plankton that lived in ancient seas. Over millions of years, these remains were buried under sediment and rock where heat and pressure slowly transformed them into oil and gas. Areas of rock where large amounts of oil and gas are trapped are known as reservoirs.

Oil exploration

Geologists look for oil and gas by studying rock formations. This can be done by a seismic survey. Sound waves are sent into the seabed from airguns. The time taken for their echoes to be reflected back is measured by detectors towed behind a boat. These measurements can indicate what lies beneath the seabed, since different kinds of rock reflect sound at different rates.

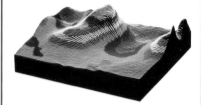

Computers can process data from a seismic survey to make a 3D picture of rock formations below the seabed.

Platforms

If a potential reservoir is discovered, test wells are drilled from drilling ships or floating platforms. If a usable reservoir is found, a production platform is built. It is now possible to build platforms taller than skyscrapers in more than 400m (1,300ft) of water. Large platforms can accommodate hundreds of workers who work in shifts to ensure non-stop production.

Drilling wells

To bring oil and gas to the surface, wells are drilled with cutting tools called drilling bits, suspended from a tower. Wells can be drilled at an angle or straight down. A system of valves controls the flow from each well. Most wells are between 900m (3,000ft) and 5,000m (16,400ft) deep.

An offshore platform may have more than 20 wells. Some reach reservoirs over 5km (3 miles) from the platform.

Offshore platform

Wells

Water

Gas

Oil

An oil and gas reservoir

Drilling bit

A drilling bit has diamond or metal teeth. It can drill at a rate of 30cm (1ft) to 60m (200ft) an hour, depending on the hardness of the rock.

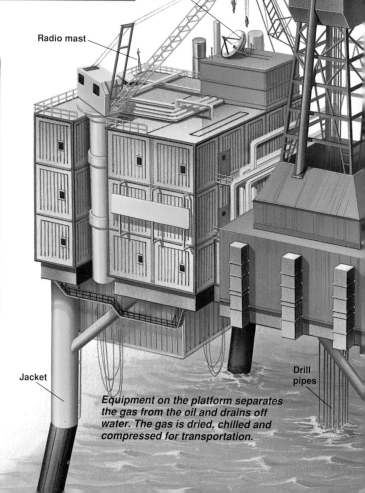

Flare in which gas that cannot be used is burned

Drilling tower or derrick

Crane for lifting supplies off ships

Satellite dish

Radio mast

Jacket

Drill pipes

Equipment on the platform separates the gas from the oil and drains off water. The gas is dried, chilled and compressed for transportation.

A platform consists of a jacket (the huge "legs" which go down to the seabed), a deck which sits on top, and various "topside" modules which contain machinery, living areas and equipment. Large platforms are assembled in stages. Some jackets have hollow legs and are floated out to sea, towed by small boats. They are upended by a controlled flooding of the legs when they arrive at the site.

Workers are brought to and from a platform by helicopter. They spend a few weeks on and then a few weeks off the platform.

The accommodation unit contains cabins, kitchens, restaurants, a gym, offices, a radio room, a sauna and a recreation room.

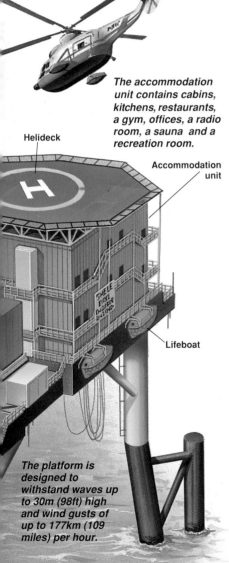

Helideck

Accommodation unit

Lifeboat

The platform is designed to withstand waves up to 30m (98ft) high and wind gusts of up to 177km (109 miles) per hour.

Processing gas and oil

Oil and gas are transported to an oil refinery or gas processing plant on land through underwater pipelines, or by very large ships called tankers. At a refinery, the oil is cleaned and broken down into usable forms, such as transport and heating fuels. At a gas processing plant, natural gas is made into fuels for heating and for cooking.

Oil and gas can be piped from a platform into a tanker at a steel structure called a single anchor leg mooring, which is secured to the seabed. The mooring is often some distance from the platform.

Renewable energy

Tides, waves and currents carry with them more than enough energy to meet the world's demand for electric power. Various devices have been designed to harness this energy, but more research is needed to make them efficient. In areas where the tidal range (the difference in height between high and low tide) is over 5m (16ft), a tidal barrage can be used to generate electricity. It holds back the rising or falling tide in an estuary, forcing water through pipes containing devices called turbines. The water spins the turbine blades, producing electricity in generators.

Tidal barrage

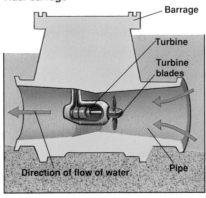

Barrage

Turbine

Turbine blades

Direction of flow of water

Pipe

Shore-based wave power devices operate on a similar principle to tidal barrages. Incoming waves force air into a narrow pipe and through a turbine. One such wave power device is being tested on the Isle of Islay in Scotland.

Shore-based wave power device

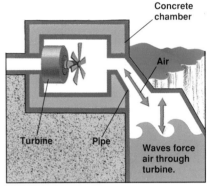

Concrete chamber

Air

Turbine   Pipe

Waves force air through turbine.

A process that could potentially tap the heat stored in the oceans is called OTEC (Ocean Thermal Energy Conversion). OTEC uses warm water at the surface to heat and vaporize ammonia. The moving vapour drives a turbine. Cold water from 900m (3,000ft) down cools and condenses the vapour so that it can be used again. OTEC would only work in seas where the surface is at least 22°C (40°F) warmer than the depths.

Plan for an OTEC plant

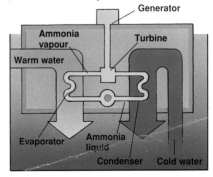

Generator

Ammonia vapour

Turbine

Warm water

Evaporator

Ammonia liquid

Condenser   Cold water

Ships and boats

Ships and boats come in all shapes and sizes, from one-person canoes to huge cruise liners that carry hundreds of passengers. The first boats set sail on the ocean at least 20,000 years ago. Now, the most important group of ships are the cargo ships that carry food, fuels, raw materials and manufactured goods from country to country. On these pages are some of the various types of ships you might see at a port. (They are not shown to scale.)

Car ferries carry passengers and vehicles for short distances, for example, across lakes and rivers, to and from islands, or across small seas such as the Adriatic and Baltic. Large ferries can transport over 2,000 passengers and more than 600 vehicles. Some have cabins where people can sleep on overnight crossings. This shows the type of ferry that sails between France and Britain.

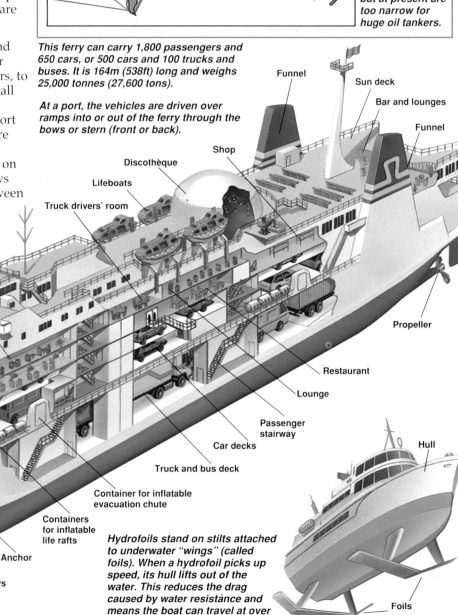

This map shows the world's main shipping routes, or lanes. Thick lines show very busy routes.

The Panama and Suez canals save some ships from a long journey around South America or Africa, but at present are too narrow for huge oil tankers.

Panama Canal

Suez Canal

Equator

This ferry can carry 1,800 passengers and 650 cars, or 500 cars and 100 trucks and buses. It is 164m (538ft) long and weighs 25,000 tonnes (27,600 tons).

At a port, the vehicles are driven over ramps into or out of the ferry through the bows or stern (front or back).

Funnel

Sun deck

Bar and lounges

Funnel

Shop

Discothèque

Lifeboats

Truck drivers' room

Lounges

Bridge - the ferry is steered from here.

Restaurant

Lounge

Passenger stairway

Car decks

Truck and bus deck

Container for inflatable evacuation chute

Containers for inflatable life rafts

Anchor

Propellers for moving sideways

The bows open up for vehicles to drive on or off.

Propeller

Hull

Hydrofoils stand on stilts attached to underwater "wings" (called foils). When a hydrofoil picks up speed, its hull lifts out of the water. This reduces the drag caused by water resistance and means the boat can travel at over 148kph (92mph).

Foils

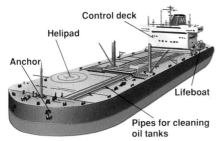

Propellers   **Cushion of air**

Hovercrafts (also called air-cushion vehicles, or ACVs) skim over the water on a cushion of air. Fans blow strong jets of air down into the cushion to keep it inflated. Propellers drive the craft forward as they spin.

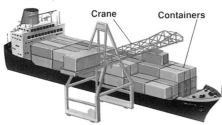

Control deck

Helipad

Anchor

Lifeboat

Pipes for cleaning oil tanks

Tankers carry oil or other liquid cargo in tanks inside their hulls. They are the largest ships that have ever been built. Some are over 20 times the length of a tennis court and can carry over 400,000 tonnes (440,000 tons) of oil.

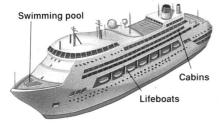

Crane   **Containers**

Container ships carry goods of all kinds in large metal boxes (containers) of a standard size. These can be loaded and unloaded quickly from trains and trucks by cranes at the side of a dock. 2,000 containers can be carried by one ship.

Swimming pool

Cabins

Lifeboats

Large ships called cruise liners take people on long sea voyages, called cruises. Cruise liners are like floating hotels. They have restaurants, dining rooms, cinemas, shops, bars, swimming pools, games rooms and even hospitals.

Cruise quiz

The map below shows the route for a world cruise. The cruise ship starts in England, visits 23 different countries and sails 35,040 nautical miles (64,824km or 40,296 miles). The black dots show the 29 ports that the cruise liner visits. Using the map, try to answer the following questions:

1. Which oceans and which canals does the liner sail through? (Use the big map on page 3 to help you.)

2. What is the compass direction of sailing from Madeira to Barbados?

3. If the liner sailed non-stop, at an average speed of 20 knots (20 nautical miles per hour), how many 24-hour "days" would be needed to complete the cruise?

Answers on page 32.

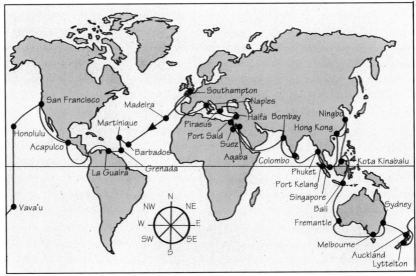

Navigation

Ships could not cross the oceans without instruments to help them navigate (find the way). In the past, navigators used a compass to tell direction, a type of clock called a chronometer to determine their longitude (east-west position) and a sextant to find their latitude (north-south position).

Modern ships have electronic navigation equipment. They may find their position by signals sent from satellites in space, or by radio signals from the shore. Radar equipment can be used to spot icebergs, rocks and other ships. It sends out radio waves and measures how long they take to bounce back off objects. Sonar is used to detect underwater objects. Light ships, lighthouses and automatic, floating navigation buoys mark paths for ships that are approaching port.

A sextant was used to measure the angle of the Sun, a planet, or a star above the horizon, to find out a ship's latitude.

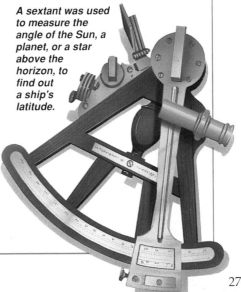

Oceans in danger

Despite the fact that seas and oceans provide us with food and energy and are useful in so many ways, some people treat them very carelessly. They use them as dumping grounds for waste, destroying habitats, poisoning sea creatures and threatening the health of the people that depend on them. So many animals and plants have been hunted or collected that some species have been driven to the point of extinction.

Pollution

Enormous quantities of pollutants enter the oceans each year. Pollution can build up in a food web when big animals eat smaller ones that have been contaminated. One of the main pollutants is oil. About 3.5 million tonnes (3.9 million tons) of it enter the oceans each year. Ten percent comes from tanker spills. The rest is due to leaks from oil fields, smaller accidents or deliberate dumping.

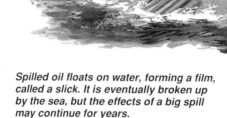

Spilled oil floats on water, forming a film, called a slick. It is eventually broken up by the sea, but the effects of a big spill may continue for years.

Oil effects

Oil is the biggest cause of seabird deaths. It may also poison plankton, fish and shellfish and the animals and people that eat them. It can smother and kill coral reefs and contaminate animals on the seabed. When oil washes up on a shore, it coats rocks and sand and kills wildlife in the intertidal zone.

If a bird tries to remove oil with its beak, it may be poisoned by oil that it swallows.

Oil clogs a bird's feathers and destroys its waterproof coating. The bird then cannot keep warm or stay afloat in the water.

Oiled shags often hold out their wings to try to "dry" them.

An oiled bird may drown, die of cold, or starve to death because it can no longer hunt and catch its food. Other animals that scavenge on the oily bodies of dead birds also swallow oil.

Spill damage

When the tanker Exxon Valdez ran aground in 1989 in Alaska, USA, it leaked about 35,000 tonnes (38,600 tons) of oil into the sea. This is thought to have killed about 400,000 seabirds, 5,500 sea otters, hundreds of seals and 22 orcas (killer whales).

A tanker called the Braer sank off the Shetland Islands, Scotland in 1993, spilling over 84,000 tonnes (92,600 tons) of oil. Local fish farms were badly affected. It will be many years before the full impact of this spill can be assessed.

Many surviving sea otters have failed to breed since the Exxon Valdez disaster because their internal organs have been damaged by oil which they swallowed.

Cleaning up oil

The extent of the damage caused by spilled oil is determined by factors such as the temperature of the water, the type of oil and the weather at the time of an accident. These are some of the methods used to try to clean up after a large spill.

Detergents are sprayed onto a slick from an aircraft to try to disperse the oil. In some cases the detergent can cause more harm to ocean life than the oil itself.

Floating plastic tubes, called booms, can be laid around an oil slick to stop it from spreading. Some of the oil can then be sucked up by machines called skimmers.

Beaches may be cleaned using suction pumps, buckets and spades, hoses, brushes and detergent. Attempts may be made to clean oil off birds and other animals.

Attempts may be made to set fire to a slick on the surface of the water and burn off the oil. The smoke from a burning slick can cause more damage than the slick itself.

Litter and sewage

Litter in the sea and on beaches is dangerous. Plastic waste, for example, kills two million seabirds, 100,000 mammals and vast numbers of turtles and fish each year. Most litter in the sea has been thrown from ships, but some is washed into the sea from rivers and beaches.

Large amounts of sewage (waste from toilets and drains) are also dumped into the sea. Sewage is 99% water but also contains bacteria and viruses. Eating fish and shellfish from sewage-polluted sea water can cause food-poisoning. The discharge of sewage near areas that are used for swimming, diving and other water sports can cause other illnesses.

Times for types of litter to be broken down by bacteria in the sea.

Paper	2-5 months
Orange peel	6 months
Milk cartons	5 years
Plastic foam	Never
Plastic bottles	50-80 years

More pollution

Many other types of pollution find their way into the oceans. Water seeping through buried rubbish can turn into a poisonous liquid that pollutes groundwater. Fertilizers and pesticides from gardens and farms can also seep into groundwater which ends up in rivers and seas.

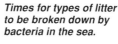

Fertilizers, pesticides and other chemicals sprayed onto crops may end up in the sea.

Waste from nuclear power stations is taken to factories, called reprocessing plants, to be treated. These plants may discharge hazardous waste water into the sea. Chemicals and poisonous metals that are used in industrial processes, may also end up in the sea when factories dispose of waste.

Drums of toxic chemicals washed up on a beach.

Plastic waste can injure and kill seabirds.

Threatened wildlife

There are many other threats to wildlife and many other species in danger. This lists just a few.

★Whales such as humpbacks and blue whales were hunted so much in the past that they may not be able to recover their numbers.

★Some species of sharks are now endangered because so many have been killed for food and sport.

★Some types of corals and shellfish are now rare because people collect them to make things such as bracelets, necklaces and ornaments.

★Turtles get caught in fishing nets and are hunted for their meat and shells. Their eggs are dug up from beaches to be sold for food. All species of sea turtles are now in danger of extinction because of this.

Saving our seas

The seas and oceans could provide a constant supply of food and energy for the world's growing population, if we made good use of them. However, unless we act now to protect the oceans, further vital habitats will be destroyed, rare species will be wiped out and many potential benefits could be lost forever.

Giant kelp is already harvested for use in the manufacture of chemicals. This fast-growing seaweed could also be a source of methane gas in the future.

Who owns the sea?

Because the world's oceans cover such vast areas, it is difficult to regulate how they are used and to determine who has control over them. The open oceans away from the coasts are considered to be a common global resource - they belong to everybody and can be used by anybody. The area up to 200 nautical miles (370km or 230 miles) around a country's shores are under the control of that country. This area is known as an Exclusive Economic Zone, or EEZ.

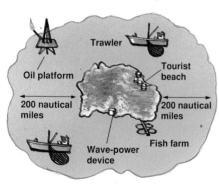

A country has a right to the fish, gas, oil and other resources found within its Exclusive Economic Zone (EEZ).

International agreements

International cooperation and legislation are needed to prevent pollution, overfishing and hunting and ensure that the ocean's harvest is shared fairly. There have been agreements among groups of countries over matters such as whaling, fishing and pollution, though legislation is difficult to enforce. No agreement has yet been made between all countries.

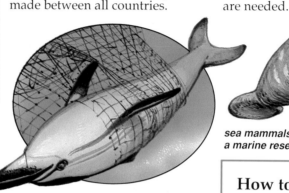

In 1991, members of the United Nations Organization (the UN) agreed to ban the use of drift nets longer than 3km (1.9 miles). These "walls of death" killed mammals and birds as well as fish.

Ecotourism

In the past 30 years, an increase in tourism has put pressure on fragile coastal habitats. Coral reefs, for example, have been damaged by divers, and mangroves have been cleared to make way for airports, ports, hotels, roads and shops.

Shells and corals are collected and sold to tourists.

Now, many countries are developing forms of tourism, often known as ecotourism, which do less damage and bring money to local people. They have found, for example, that tourists will pay to visit unspoiled habitats with guides who ensure they do no damage.

Marine reserves

One way of preventing the destruction of marine habitats is to create nature reserves in the sea. In these areas wildlife is protected and human activities, such as diving, sailing and fishing, are controlled or banned completely. The largest marine reserve is the Great Barrier Reef. Many more such reserves are needed.

Manatees are endangered sea mammals. They are now protected in a marine reserve in Florida, USA.

How to help

These are some of the things you can do to help save the seas. Remember that even if you live far from a coast, your waste water may end up in the sea.

★Use phosphate-free products for cleaning and washing. Phosphates in water cause algae to multiply, starving the water of oxygen and killing animals.

★Make less waste water. Take showers instead of baths, if possible. Turn off the water while you brush your teeth.

★If you have a garden, try to avoid using weedkillers, pesticides and other chemicals which can pollute groundwater.

★Do not collect seashells or buy things made from shells, coral or tortoiseshell (from sea turtles). Do not eat turtle eggs or soup.

★Join one of the national or local groups which campaign to clean up beaches and oceans and work to protect wildlife.

Glossary

Abyssal plain. The ocean floor beyond the **continental shelf** where the average depth of the sea is about 4,000m (13,100ft).

Asthenosphere. A layer of hot rock in the Earth's **mantle**, at a depth of 80 to 200km (50 to 125 miles).

Atoll. A ring-shaped or horseshoe-shaped coral reef.

Baleen. A fringe of tough bristles inside the mouths of some whales and sharks, used to strain **plankton** from the water.

Constructive wave. A wave that carries sand, shingle or pebbles onto the shore and gradually builds up the beach.

Continental shelf. The seabed and the area of an ocean nearest the land, where the sea is less than 350m (1,150ft) deep.

Continental slope. A steep slope at the edge of a **continental shelf**.

Coral polyp. A small sea animal. Over thousands of years, coral reefs form from the skeletons of dead coral polyps.

Core. The central part of the Earth below the **mantle**, consisting of nickel and iron.

Coriolis effect. Effect caused by the Earth's rotation which deflects **prevailing winds** and currents to the right in the northern hemisphere or to the left in the southern hemisphere.

Crust. The outer layer of the Earth.

Deposition. The process by which the sea, rivers or glaciers deposit mud, sand or pebbles, forming features such as beaches.

Destructive wave. A wave that contributes to the **erosion** of a coast.

Echo-sounding. A method used to survey and map undersea landscapes or to find fish by sending pulses of sound into the water or down to the seabed.

EEZ. Exclusive Economic Zone. An area stretching 200 nautical miles (370km or 230 miles) from the shores of a country which only that country can exploit.

El Niño. A warm current that sometimes occurs off the west coast of South America.

Erosion. The gradual wearing away of the surface of the land by rain, waves, rivers, wind and ice.

Evaporation. A process by which a liquid changes into a gas, or vapour.

Fetch. The distance of open sea water over which a wind blows to create waves.

Food web. The way in which plants and animals are connected through food.

Global warming. An increase in world temperature which may be caused by heat being trapped by gases such as carbon dioxide.

Groundwater. Water under the ground. Most groundwater is rain water that has seeped down from the surface.

Guyot (also called a **tablemount**). A flat-topped **seamount**.

Gyre. A vast circle of moving water in the open ocean made from the paths of a number of currents.

Hurricane. See **Tropical cyclone**.

Hydrothermal vent. A hot, mineral-rich spring at an **ocean ridge** in the deep oceans.

Intertidal zone. The part of a shore that is underwater at high tide and exposed to the air at low tide.

Island arc. A curved line of volcanic islands.

Lithosphere. The Earth's **crust** and the upper part of the **mantle**. The lithosphere is thought to consist of **plates**.

Longshore drift (US = **longshore flow**). The movement of sand or stones along a shore, caused by waves meeting the shore at an angle.

Magma. Molten (melted) rock inside the Earth.

Mangrove swamp. An area of tropical, swampy land near a coast or in an estuary, where mangrove trees grow.

Mantle. A layer of dense rock between the Earth's **crust** and **core**.

Neap tide. A very low **tidal range** that occurs when the Moon and Sun are at right angles to one another.

Oceanography. The scientific study of seas and oceans.

Ocean ridge. A long, undersea mountain range where two **plates** of the **lithosphere** are moving apart.

Ocean trench. A deep undersea valley where two **plates** are moving together and one is descending beneath the other.

Photosynthesis. The process by which plants use the energy in sunlight to make food for themselves from water, carbon dioxide and minerals.

Plankton. Tiny plants and animals that drift in the sea.

Plate. One of the huge blocks that comprise the Earth's **lithosphere**. Plates fit together like enormous jigsaw pieces.

Prevailing wind. The most common wind that tends to blow in a particular area.

Radar. A device on a ship that uses radio waves to detect objects such as rocks and other ships.

ROV. Remote Operated Vehicle. A small, unmanned robot, used for undersea work.

SCUBA. Self-contained Underwater Breathing Apparatus.

Seamount. An isolated volcanic mountain on the ocean floor that does not break the surface of the sea.

Seismic survey. A method of investigating the rocks and sediments under the seabed or under the ground, using sound waves or shock waves.

Sonar. A system for detecting underwater objects or animals with reflected sound.

Spring tide. Very low and very high tides that occur when the Earth, Moon and Sun line up at new and full moons.

Storm surge. A rise in the normal sea level in a particular area of the ocean when a storm occurs at the same time as a high tide.

Submersible. A small submarine that usually stays underwater for less than a day.

Tidal barrage. A structure built across an estuary to generate electricity, using the energy of rising and falling tides.

Tidal barrier. A structure built across a river to protect a town or city from tidal flooding.

Tidal range. The difference in water height between high tide and low tide.

Tropical cyclone (also called a **hurricane**). A huge, circular storm with strong winds and heavy rain that develops over warm oceans.

Tsunami. A wave caused by a large underwater earthquake or volcanic eruption.

Water vapour. Water in the form of a gas in the air, as a result of **evaporation**.

Index

Answers to quiz on page 27

1. Atlantic, Pacific and Indian Oceans, Panama and Suez Canals
2. Southwest
3. 73 days

Acknowledgements

Page 6: photo of Alvin © Woods Hole Oceanographic Institution/Rod Catanach
Page 10: photo of Thames Barrier © National Rivers Authority
Page 17: ATSR satellite image © SERC's Rutherford Appleton Laboratory; satellite image of Hurricane Gilbert © HMSO
Page 24: computer image from seismic survey © Shell U.K. Ltd

The publishers are grateful to the following organizations for provision of information and materials for use as artists' reference: Benthos Undersea Systems Technology, NERC's Institute of Oceanographic Sciences, Deacon Laboratory, The Marine Conservation Society, Slingsby Engineering Limited, Sealink Stena Line, Thames Barrier Visitors Centre, Woods Hole Oceanographic Institution, W.S.Ocean Systems.